D0810404

THE POWER OF
THINKING BIG

by

John C. Maxwell

RIVER
OAK
PUBLISHING

All quotations without attribution are assumed to be anonymous.

The Power of Thinking Big
ISBN 1-58919-408-X
Copyright © 2001 by John C. Maxwell

Published by RiverOak Publishing
P.O. Box 700143
Tulsa, Oklahoma 74170-0143

Introduction

Mark Twain once said, "Take your mind out every now and then and dance on it. It is getting all caked up." That was his way of saying, "Try something new, break new ground, get out of your rut."

This is good advice for all of us. Sometimes we need something to jolt us out of a lifeless routine—a bold new thought, a different slant on a familiar subject, or a bit of wisdom from someone who's "walked down that road" before we have.

The quotes in this book have been selected to inspire you to see life from a different angle. Many contain a little barb or twist to get your attention. Some will make you laugh; others will make you think— think big! I hope that they will equip you to make your world better tomorrow than it is today.

After all, you never know when you will discover that big thought that will change your life!

—John C. Maxwell

Thinking in its lower grades is
comparable to paper money, and in
its higher forms it is a kind of poetry

—Havelock Ellis

There is nothing either good or bad,
but thinking makes it so.

—Shakespeare

Every person who has become
successful has simply formed the
habit of doing things that failures
dislike doing and will not do.

—John C. Maxwell

Never let go of a dream
until you're ready to wake
up and make it happen.

_____

It takes all the running you can do to
keep in the same place. If you want
to get somewhere else, you must
run at least twice as fast as that!

—The Queen of Hearts in
Alice in Wonderland

Practice doesn't make perfect—
it makes permanent.

—John C. Maxwell

Heart is what separates
the good from the great.

—Michael Jordan

One difference between
perseverance and obstinacy is that
one often comes from a strong will,
and the other from a strong won't.

—Henry Ward Beecher

Your attitude is either your best friend
or your worst enemy, your greatest
asset or your greatest liability.

—John C. Maxwell

Don't just learn something
from every experience;
learn something positive.

—Allen H. Neuharth

_____

When you're through
changing, you're through.

—Bruce Barton

People are changed, not
by coercion or intimidation,
but by example.

—John C. Maxwell

In a small town, an old codger
lived in the same house for nearly
fifty years. One day he surprised
everyone by moving next door.
When asked why he moved, he said,
"I guess it's just the gypsy in me."

It's not the mountain
we conquer, but ourselves.

—Edmund Hillary
First to climb Mt. Everest

Are you bored with life?
Maybe your expecter has expired.

—John C. Maxwell

There are no shortcuts
to anyplace worth going.

—Beverly Sills

_____

One definition of insanity is
to believe that you can keep
doing what you've been doing
and get different results.

Stop trying to grow your organization.
Work on people's attitudes. If you do
that, your organization will experience
10 percent growth overnight.

—John C. Maxwell

It pays to plan ahead. It wasn't
raining when Noah built the ark.

_____

I not only use all the brains
I have, but all I can borrow.

— Woodrow Wilson

Leadership determines the
direction of the company.
Organization determines
the potential of the company.
Personnel determine the
success of the company.

—John C. Maxwell

Ideas won't keep: something
must be done about them.

—Alfred North Whitehead

You've got to get up every morning
with determination if you're going
to go to bed with satisfaction.

—George Horace Lorimer

Pay now, play later;
play now, pay later.

—John C. Maxwell

The best cure for a sluggish
mind is to disturb its routine.

—William H. Danforth

He who is good at making
excuses is seldom good
for anything else.

—Benjamin Franklin

We first form habits.
Then habits form us.

—John C. Maxwell

Most people want to change the
world to improve their lives. What
a wasted effort. If they would only
improve themselves, they would be
better off and so would the world.

In youth we want to change the world.
In old age we want to change youth.

—Garth Henrichs

People stop growing
when the price gets too high.

—John C. Maxwell

The richest soil, uncultivated,
produces the rankest weeds.

—Plutarch

Any time the going seems
easier, better check and see
if you're not going downhill.

Image is what people think we are.
Integrity is what we really are.

—John C. Maxwell

Every generation needs
a new revolution.

—Thomas Jefferson

If you're not doing something
with your life, it doesn't
matter how long it is.

—Peace Corps Commercial

If your vision doesn't
cost you something,
it's a daydream.

—John C. Maxwell

When you don't want to do
something, one excuse
is as good as another.

_____

Ninety-nine percent of failures
come from people who have
the habit of making excuses.

—George Washington Carver

Our attitude at the beginning of
a task will affect its outcome
more than anything else.

—John C. Maxwell

You can impress people
at a distance, but you can
impact them only up close.

—Howard Hendricks

———————————

Our strength is seen in the things
we stand for; our weakness is
seen in the things we fall for.

—Theodore Epp

If people respect you but don't like you,
they won't stay with you. If they like
you but don't respect you, they'll stay
with you, but they won't follow you.
To be an effective leader, you must
earn both from your people.

—John C. Maxwell

One-fifth of the people are
against everything all the time.

—Robert Kennedy

_____

I am only one, but I am one. I cannot
do everything, but I can do something.
And that which I can do,
by the grace of God, I will do.

—Dwight L. Moody

Your attitude is the eye of your soul.
If your attitude is negative, then you
see things negatively. If it's positive,
then you see things positively.

—John C. Maxwell

We judge ourselves by what we
feel capable of doing; others
judge us by what we have done.

—Henry Wadsworth Longfellow

It's right to be content with what you
have, never with what you are.

You cannot go any higher
than your self-image.

—John C. Maxwell

No reserve, no retreat,

and no regrets.

—Bill Bordon,
missionary to China
written on his death bed

Never retreat in the face of difficulties.

Advance as conditions permit.

If conditions don't permit,

create those conditions.

A difficult crisis can be more readily
endured if we retain the conviction
that our existence holds a purpose—
a cause to pursue, a person
to love, a goal to achieve.

—John C. Maxwell

Before putting off until tomorrow
something you can do today,
study it closely. Maybe you
can postpone it indefinitely.

———————————

Don't put off for tomorrow what you
can do today, because if you enjoy it
today, you can do it again tomorrow.

—James A. Michener

A procrastinator puts off until
tomorrow the things he has
already put off until today.

—John C. Maxwell

Do what you can, with
what you have, where you are.

—Theodore Roosevelt

_____

When you cease to make a
contribution, you begin to die.

—Eleanor Roosevelt

The true test of stewardship is
not what your money is doing
for you but what it's doing to you.

—John C. Maxwell

Safe living generally
makes for regrets later on.

_____

You miss 100 percent of
the shots you never take.

—Wayne Gretzky

The greatest mistake we make
is living in constant fear
that we will make one.

—John C. Maxwell

Make no small plans, for they
have no capacity to stir men's souls.

The future belongs to people
who see possibilities before
they become obvious.

—Ted Levitt

Problems are those things we see
when we take our eyes off the goal.

—John C. Maxwell

I will go anywhere as
long as it's forward.

—David Livingstone

_____

The man who starts out going
nowhere, generally gets there.

—Dale Carnegie

Vision adds value to everything.

—John C. Maxwell

Opportunities are seldom labeled.

—John A. Shedd

_____

The desire for safety stands against
every great and noble enterprise.

What I *perceive* ... determines
what I *receive* ... which
determines how I *achieve.*

−John C. Maxwell

It takes less time to do
a thing right than to explain
why you did it wrong.

—Henry Wadsworth Longfellow

_____

Between saying and doing,
many a pair of shoes is worn out.

—Italian Proverb

People do what people see.
They forget your words
but follow your footsteps.

—John C. Maxwell

If you want to make enemies,
try to change something.

—Woodrow Wilson

Do not follow where the path may
lead. Follow God, instead, to where
there is no path and leave a trail.

Leading others takes courage.
Knowing the right decision is
usually easy. *Making* the
right decision is hard.

—John C. Maxwell

The hottest places in Hell are reserved
for those who in time of great moral
crises maintain their neutrality.

———————————————

Why not go out on a limb?
Isn't that where the fruit is?

—Frank Scully

Leading followers is fast and
easy, and it has little return;
leading leaders is slow and
hard, and it has a great return.

—John C. Maxwell

People who never do any more
than they get paid for, never get
paid for any more than they do.

—Elbert Hubbard

_____

People who live for themselves
are in a mighty small business.

Winners concentrate on winning;
losers concentrate on getting by.

—John C. Maxwell

Keep away from people who belittle
your ambitions. Small people always
do that, but the really great make you
feel that you, too, can become great.

—Mark Twain

Consider how hard it is to change
yourself and you'll understand
what little chance you have of
trying to change others.

—Jacob M. Braude

Loving people precedes leading them. People don't care how much you know until they know how much you care.

—John C. Maxwell

The difficulties of life are intended
to make us better—not bitter.

Life doesn't do anything to you.
It only reveals your spirit.

Hurting people hurt other people.
Once you learn this, it's easier
to "turn the other cheek."

—John C. Maxwell

Are you gonna get
any better, or is this it?

—Earl Weaver
Baltimore Orioles Manager—to an umpire

A rut is a grave with
both ends knocked out.

If you need the people,
you can't lead the people.
A co-dependent relationship
seldom grows or moves forward.

—John C. Maxwell

Men will never cast away their
dearest pleasures upon the drowsy
request of someone who does not
even seem to mean what he says.

———————————————

Don't ever be afraid to admit you
were wrong. It's like saying you're
wiser today than you were yesterday.

Every change in human attitude
must come through internal
understanding and acceptance.
Man is the only known creature
who can reshape and remold
himself by altering his attitude.

—John C. Maxwell

Time is neutral; but it can be
made the ally of those who
will seize it and use it to the full.

—Winston Churchill

_____

Essentially there are two actions
in life. Performance and excuses.
Make a decision as to which
you will accept for yourself.

—Stephen Brown

The leader's growth determines
the people's growth.

—John C. Maxwell

Great minds have purposes;
others have wishes.

—Washington Irving

Never give up, for that is
just the place and time
that the tide will turn.

—Harriet Beecher Stowe

It's lonely at the top ... so you'd
better know why you're there.

—John C. Maxwell

Excellence is the gradual result
of always striving to do better.

—Pat Riley

———————————

A good heart is better than
all the heads in the world.

—Edward Bulwer-Lytton

It's wonderful when the people
believe in their leader; it's more
wonderful when the leader
believes in the people.

—John C. Maxwell

Only the person who has
faith in himself is able
to be faithful to others.

—Erich Fromm

Learning what you cannot
do is more important than
knowing what you can do.

—Lucille Ball

Leadership functions on the
basis of trust. When trust is gone,
the leader soon will be.

—John C. Maxwell

When was the last time that you
did something for the first time?

Ninety percent of the work
done in this country is done
by people who don't feel well.

—Theodore Roosevelt

Nothing is as hard as it looks;
everything is more rewarding
than you expect; and if anything
can go right it will and at
the best possible moment.

—Maxwell's Law

Difficulties mastered are
opportunities won.

—Winston Churchill

Commitment in the face of
conflict produces character.

People buy into the leader
before they buy into the
leader's vision. If you want to
lead, you must sell yourself.

—John C. Maxwell

Anyone who has made a
mistake and doesn't correct it,
is making another one.

You never have to
recover from a good start.

Admit your failures quickly and
humbly. The people already know
when you've erred, but they'll
appreciate your right spirit.

—John C. Maxwell

The harder you work,
the harder it is to surrender.

—Vince Lombardi

_____

Persistence is stubbornness
with a purpose.

—Rich DeVos

Never take shortcuts.
They don't pay off in the long run.

—John C. Maxwell

One cannot leap a chasm in two jumps.

—Winston Churchill

Read the best books first,
or you may not have
a chance to read them at all.

—Henry David Thoreau

Where there is no hope
in the future, there is
no power in the present.

—John C. Maxwell

God never puts anyone
in a place too small to grow.

_____

Christians are supposed not
merely to endure change, nor
even profit by it, but to cause it.

—Harry Emerson Fosdick

I teach what I know, but
I reproduce what I am.

—John C. Maxwell

Your friends will stretch your
vision or choke your dream.

_____

Look carefully at the closest
associations in your life, for that
is the direction you are heading.

People are your only appreciable asset.

—John C. Maxwell

Life is a lot like tennis—the one
who can serve best seldom loses.

———————————

The measure of a life, after all, is
not its duration but its donation.

—Corrie Ten Boom

Leadership is servanthood.
Observance of this truth
keeps your motives pure and
protects you from ambition.
It also makes you like Jesus.

—John C. Maxwell

When God measures man,
he puts the tape around
his heart, not his head.

———————————

If you think you can, you can.
And if you think you can't, you're right.

—Mary Kay Ash

Problems are not our problems.
It's not what happens *to* you but
what happens *in* you that matters.

—John C. Maxwell

Experience is knowing
a lot of things you shouldn't do.

—William Knudson

_____

The young man knows the rules, but
the old man knows the exceptions.

—Oliver Wendell Holmes

Most people are educated way
beyond their level of obedience.

—John C. Maxwell

Progress always involves risks.
You can't steal second and
keep your foot on first.

—Fredrick Wilcox

_____

All life is the management
of risk, not its elimination.

—Walter Wriston

Timing is everything. The right
set-up will keep an organization
from having a wrong setback.

—John C. Maxwell

The difference between what we do and what we are capable of doing would suffice to solve most of the world's problems.

—Mahatma Gandhi

_____

If we did all the things we are capable of doing, we would literally astonish ourselves.

—Thomas Edison

To lead others to do right is wonderful.
To do right and then lead them
is more wonderful . . . and harder.

—John C. Maxwell

A determined person is one who,
when they get to the end of their
rope, ties a knot and hangs on.

—Joe L. Griffith

Above all, try something.

—Franklin D. Roosevelt

God chooses what we go through;
we choose how we go through it.

—John C. Maxwell

Nobody gets to run the mill by
doing run-of-the-mill work.

—Thomas J. Frye

You have to give up to go up.

—David Jeremiah

Respect is vital to a leader.
Without it, no one follows.
Title or position will not help it.
With it, everyone follows, and
title or position are not needed.

—John C. Maxwell

I make progress by having people
around me who are smarter than
I am—and listening to them. And I
assume that everyone is smarter
about something than I am.

—Henry Kaiser

Progress is a tide. If we stand still we
will surely be drowned. To stay on
the crest, we have to keep moving.

—Harold Mayfield

Those closest to the leader determine
his level of success or failure.
Mentoring potential leaders insures
the leader and the organization of
reaching their potential.

—John C. Maxwell

My God-given talent is my
ability to stick with something
longer than anyone else.

—Herschel Walker,
Heisman Trophy winner

A great man stands on God.

—Ralph Waldo Emerson

The gift is greater than the leader.
God's anointing upon our lives
points to His greatness, not ours.

—John C. Maxwell

Never, never stop growing. Plateaus should only be found in geography books, not in personal experience.

One who gains strength by overcoming obstacles possesses the only strength which can overcome adversity.

—Albert Schweitzer

Leading people is a responsibility,
not a perk. To whomever much
is given, much is required.

—John C. Maxwell

Life is 10 percent what you make
it and 90 percent how you take it.

—Irving Berlin

_____

To err is human . . . but when
the eraser wears out ahead of
the pencil, you're overdoing it.

—Jerry Jenkins

Jesus is my best friend. At times
I have failed people. At times people
have failed me. Jesus never fails.

—John C. Maxwell

There are a lot of ways to
become a failure, but never taking
a chance is the most successful.

————————————————

Life is like a taxi. The meter just keeps
a-ticking whether you are getting
somewhere or just standing still.

—Lou Erickson

You are only an attitude
away from success!

—John C. Maxwell

Make sure the thing you're
living for is worth dying for.

—Charles Mays

_____

People will work eight hours a
day for pay, ten hours a day for
a good boss, and twenty-four
hours a day for a good cause!

Success isn't accumulating
possessions, wealth, or power.
Success is obeying God. It means
having those closest to you
love and respect you the most.

—John C. Maxwell

The chief way you and I are disloyal
to Christ is when we make small
what He intended to make large.

—Stanley Jones

_____

When someone puts a limit on
what you will do, that person has
put a limit on what you *can* do.

See your people as they
could be, not as they are.

—John C. Maxwell

Don't think much of a person
who is not wiser today than
he was yesterday.

———————————————

Most of the things worth doing in
the world had been declared
impossible before they were done.

—Louis D. Brandeis

The next time you go looking for
a book written by an expert, find
out if the author's ever actually
done what he's proposing.

—John C. Maxwell

Most people spend more time
planning Christmas than
they do planning their lives.

Very often a change of self
is needed more than
a change of scene.

—Benson

The attitude of your people is
a reflection of *your* attitude.

—John C. Maxwell

When the eagles are silent,
the parrots begin to jabber.

— Winston Churchill

Often a leader's greatest challenge
is dealing with the multitudes of
people oblivious to the obvious.

Pastors shouldn't preach another
sermon until the people
they lead do what they've been
asked to do in the last one.

—John C. Maxwell

World records are only borrowed.

—Sebastian Coe,
British Middle-distance runner

If something has been done a
particular way for fifteen or twenty
years, it's a pretty good sign, in
these changing times, that it is
being done the wrong way.

—Elliot M. Estes

The question is not,
"Are you going to fail?"
The question is,
"How are you going
to handle your failure?"

—John C. Maxwell

If at first you do succeed,
try something harder.

———————————————

Success in life comes not from
holding a good hand, but in
playing a poor hand well.

—Denis Waitley and Rem L. Witt

Life is not a dress rehearsal.

—John C. Maxwell

We are living in days of change.
My grandfather had a farm. My father
had a garden. But I've got a can opener.

———————————————

We cannot become what we need
to be by remaining what we are.

Get a life of your own. Where's the
joy in inheriting someone else's?

—John C. Maxwell

If in the last few years you
haven't discarded a major opinion
or acquired a new one, check
your pulse. You may be dead.

—Gelett Burgess

Any business or industry that
pays equal rewards to its goof-offs
and its eager-beavers sooner or
later will find itself with more
goof-offs than eager-beavers.

—Mike Delaney

"Average" has become so bad that
a person can just show up to go
to the head of the class.

—John C. Maxwell

Most people are more
comfortable with old problems
than with new solutions.

_____

Be willing to give up all
that you now are to be
all that you can become.

Growth is a process.
Death may be automatic,
but growth is not.

—John C. Maxwell

We know what happens to
people who stay in the middle
of the road; they get run over.

—Aneurin Bevan

Deliberation is the work of many men.
Action, of one alone.

—Charles DeGaulle

If you keep doing what you've always done, you'll always get what you've always gotten.

—John C. Maxwell

The average person goes to
his grave with his music still in him.

—Oliver Wendell Holmes

Most of us must learn a great
deal every day in order to keep
ahead of what we forget.

—Frank A. Clark

You cannot overestimate
the unimportance of
practically everything.

—John C. Maxwell

All accomplishment comes
from daring to begin.

_____

Eighty percent of success
is showing up.

—Woody Allen

Many people go far in life
because someone else
thought they could.

—John C. Maxwell

If you're looking for a big opportunity,
seek out a big problem.

The fewer the words,
the better the prayer.

—Martin Luther

If you want to help others,
don't just know your faith—
show your faith.

—John C. Maxwell

No man ever listened
himself out of a job.

—Calvin Coolidge

_____

Everyone must row
with the oars he has.

—English Proverb

Circumstances do not make
you what you are ...
they reveal what you are!

—John C. Maxwell

Walk so close to God that you
leave no room for the devil.

_____

If you don't do your homework,
you won't make your free throws.

—Larry Bird

Are you feeling far from God?
Guess who moved?

—John C. Maxwell

He who never walks except
where he sees other men's tracks
will make no discoveries.

———————————

If your horse is dead, for
goodness sake—dismount!

—Eddy Ketchursid

To go nowhere, follow the crowd.

—John C. Maxwell

Restlessness is discontent—
and discontent is the first
necessity of progress. Show me
a thoroughly satisfied man—
and I will show you a failure.

—Thomas Edison

Inspiration without perspiration is
a daydream; perspiration without
inspiration is a nightmare.

Any time you let up,
expect a letdown.

—John C. Maxwell

The reasonable man adapts himself to the world; the unreasonable one persists in trying to adapt the world to himself. Therefore all progress depends on the unreasonable man.

—George Bernard Shaw

The world is moving so fast these days that the man who says it can't be done is generally interrupted by someone doing it.

—Elbert Hubbard

People are like rubber bands:
They must be stretched
to be effective.

—John C. Maxwell

The reason so many people never
get anywhere in life is because, when
opportunity knocks, they are out in the
backyard looking for four-leaf clovers.

—Walter P. Chrysler

Everything comes to him
who hustles while he waits.

—Thomas Edison

Leadership development is a lifetime
journey—not a weekend trip.

—John C. Maxwell

You have never tested God's
resources until you have
attempted the impossible.

———————————

Achievers are not only persistent,
they are also hard workers
who believe in themselves.

—Timothy L. Griffith

Whiners achieve only when they
feel like it. Winners achieve
even when they don't.

−John C. Maxwell

A thoroughbred horse never
looks at the other horses.
It just concentrates on
running the fastest race it can.

—Henry Fonda

The farsighted tend to get
blindsided by the nearsighted.

Those who follow the crowd
will never be followed by a crowd.

—John C. Maxwell

If we study the giants,
we are less apt to be pygmies.

You must have long-range goals
to keep you from being
frustrated by short-range failures.

—Charles C. Noble

Decisions are made in
a moment, but growth
comes from daily discipline.

—John C. Maxwell

About the Author

John Maxwell is one of the world's most respected authorities on leadership and personal effectiveness. He has written more than twenty books, including the *New York Times* best seller *The 21 Irrefutable Laws of Leadership,* which has sold more than half a million copies. In addition to his writing career, he is a popular speaker, inspiring more than 250,000 people annually at appearances nationwide.

Dr. Maxwell's advice is based on his thirty-plus years of experience as a pastoral and organizational leader. He is founder of the INJOY Group, an organization that helps people maximize their personal and leadership potential. And he has served as a senior pastor for churches in California, Ohio, and Indiana.

The father of two grown children, Dr. Maxwell lives in Atlanta, Georgia, with Margaret, his wife of more than twenty-five years.

Want to Increase Your Influence?

Additional copies of this book and other titles by John C. Maxwell
are available from your local bookstore.

The Power of Leadership
The Power of Attitude
The Power of Influence

RIVER
OAK
PUBLISHING